**Lemur-tail
sea horse**
(Hippocampus mohnikei)

**Short-headed
sea horse**
(Hippocampus breviceps)

**Barbour's
sea horse**
(Hippocampus barbouri)

**Zebra
sea horse**
(Hippocampus zebra)

**Long-snouted
sea horse**
(Hippocampus guttulatus)

**Great
sea horse**
(Hippocampus kelloggi)

The author, illustrator, and publisher would like to thank
Colin Wells of the National Marine Aquarium in Plymouth, England,
for his expert advice and guidance during the preparation of this book.

First U.S. paperback edition with CD 2010

Library of Congress Cataloging-in-Publication Data is available.
Library of Congress Catalog Card Number 2005050755
ISBN 978-0-7636-2989-2 (hardcover)
ISBN 978-0-7636-4140-5 (paperback)
ISBN 978-0-7636-4650-9 (paperback with CD)
14 13 12 11 10 09
SWT
10 9 8 7 6 5 4 3 2 1

Printed in Dongguan, Guangdong, China

This book was typeset in Lawrence.
The illustrations were made from vinyl engravings,
watercolor washes, and printed wood textures.

Candlewick Press
99 Dover Street
Somerville, Massachusetts 02144

visit us at www.candlewick.com

For Margaret
C. B.

For Dominic
J. L.

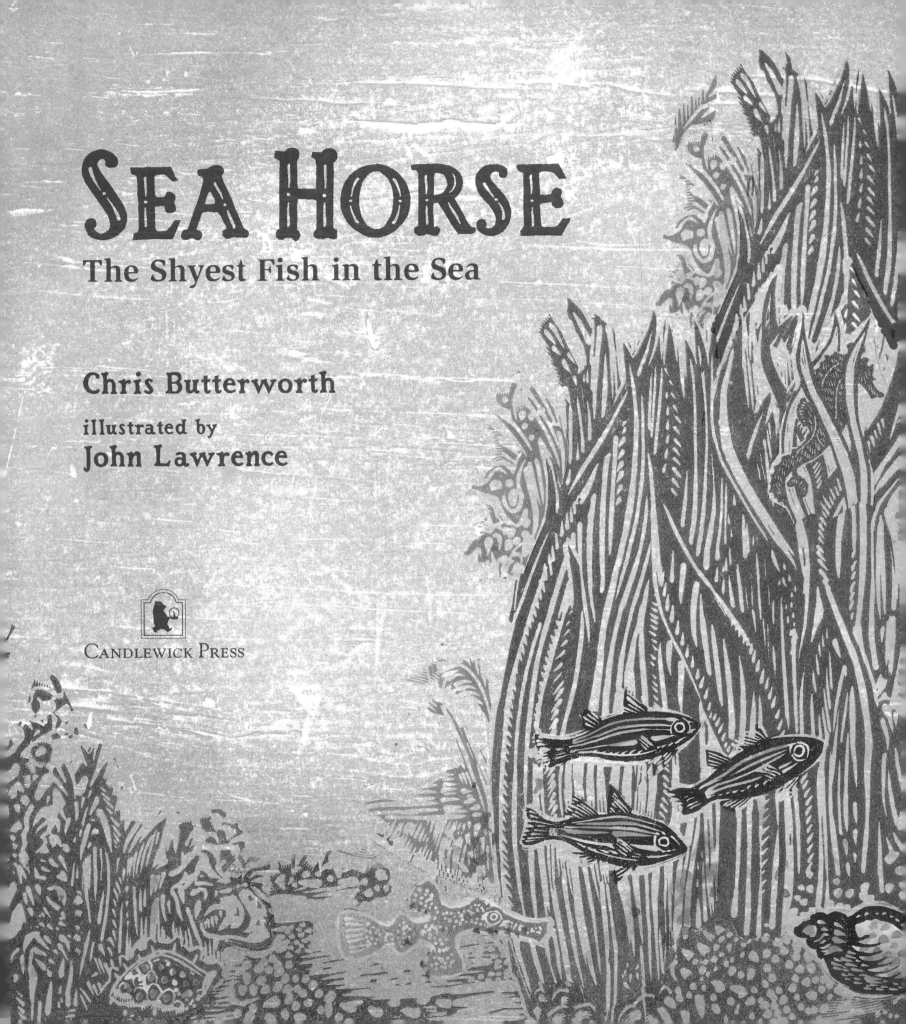

SEA HORSE

The Shyest Fish in the Sea

Chris Butterworth

illustrated by
John Lawrence

CANDLEWICK PRESS

In the warm ocean, among the waving
sea-grass meadows, an eye like a small black bead
is watching the fish dart by.
Who does it belong to?

6

SEA HORSE—
one of the shyest
fish in the sea.

Sea Horse has a head
like a horse,
a tail like a monkey, and
a pouch like a kangaroo.

This one is a Barbour's sea horse.
He has tiny prickles down his back, like a dragon.
He may not look much like a fish . . . but that's what he is.

For a long time, no one was sure what kind of animal the sea horse was.
Its scientific name is **Hippocampus**, which means "horselike sea monster."

Sea Horse swims
upright. He moves
himself through
the water with the little
fins on his head and
the larger one
on his back.

He can only
swim slowly,
so if a hungry
snapper cruises by,
looking for a snack,
Sea Horse does
something very
clever:
he holds still and
changes color (now you see him . . .)

Sea horses have hard bony ridges all down their bodies.
Not many other creatures eat sea horses—probably because they're just too difficult to swallow.

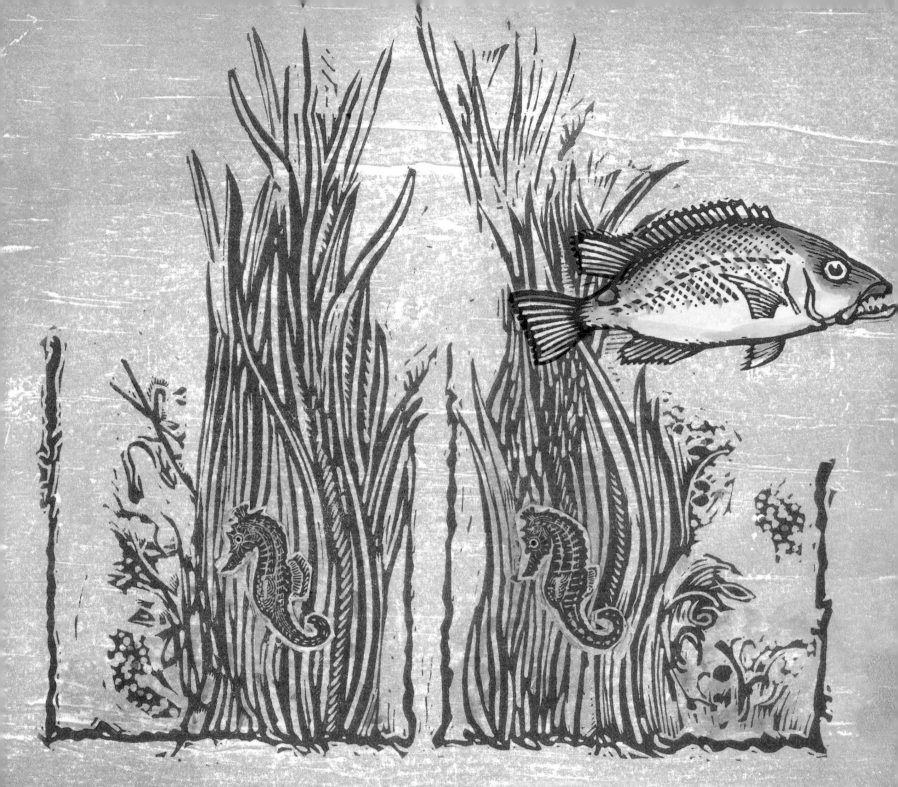

until he's almost invisible   **(now you don't!).**

The way sea horses change the color of their skin to blend in with
their surroundings is called camouflage.

Every day at sunrise,
Sea Horse swims slowly off
to meet his mate.

They twist their tails together and twirl gently around,
changing color until they match.

Sea horses are faithful to one mate and often pair up for life.

Today Sea Horse's mate
is full of ripe eggs.

The two of them dance till sunset,
and then she puts her eggs into his pouch.

Barbour's sea horses mate every few weeks during the breeding season.
Only the male sea horse has a pouch. Only the female sea horse can grow eggs.

Sea Horse sways about
to get the eggs settled in,
then seals his pouch
shut tight.

Sea horses are the
only male fish to get
"pregnant" like this,
growing their young
inside their
own bodies.

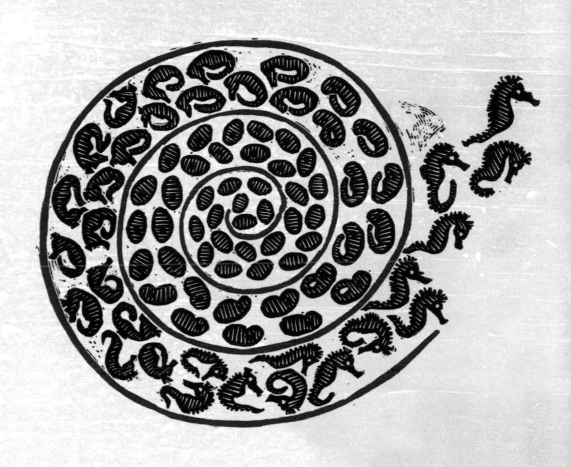

Safe inside, the dots in the eggs
begin to grow into baby
sea horses. They break out
of their eggs and keep on growing,
every one with a head like
a tiny horse and a tail like
a tiny monkey.

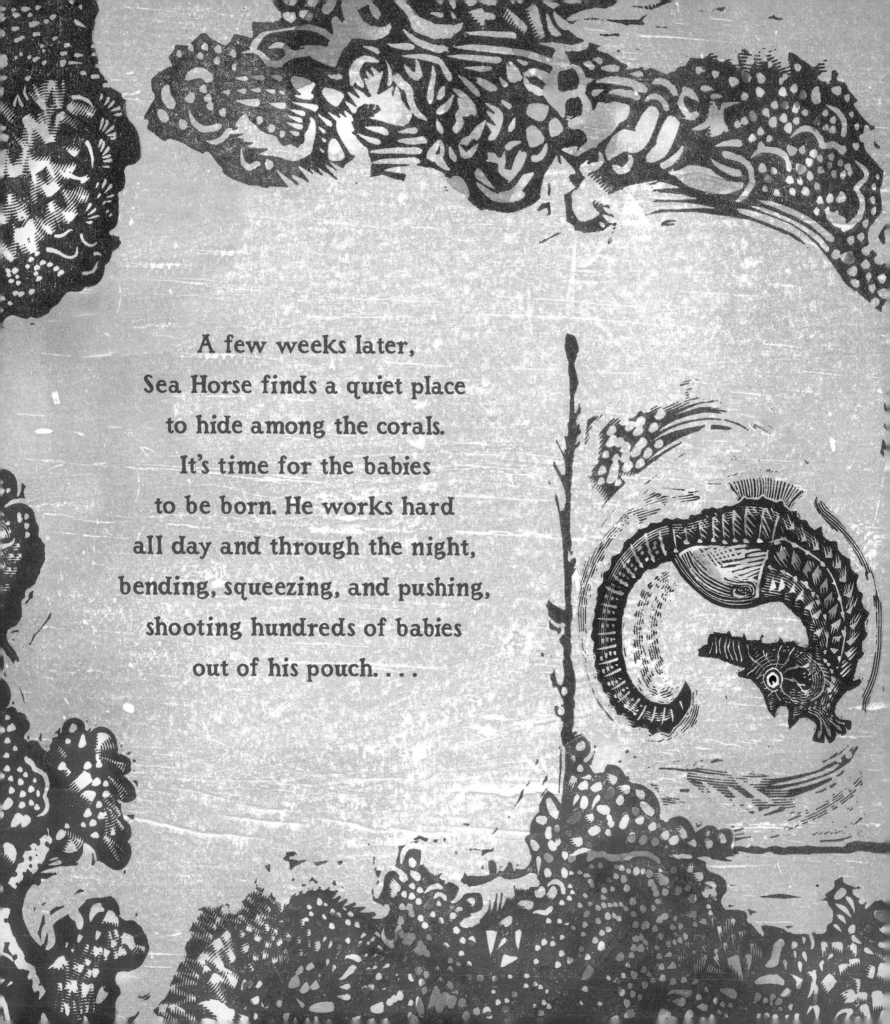

A few weeks later,
Sea Horse finds a quiet place
to hide among the corals.
It's time for the babies
to be born. He works hard
all day and through the night,
bending, squeezing, and pushing,
shooting hundreds of babies
out of his pouch. . . .

Barbour's sea horses can have two to three hundred babies at one time.

They swirl around him
in the water like smoke.

One or two of the babies hang on to Dad's nose for a while
(it's the first and biggest thing they've seen),

Each tiny new sea horse is a perfect copy of its parents and is ready for life on its own as soon as it's born.

but when they let go . . . they are so tiny and light that the current soon floats them away.

This new sea horse
is only as long
as your eyelash,
but she can find her
own food right away.
Her eyes move separately
from each other
(one can peer up while
the other looks down),
so she can spot
food coming from
any direction.

Sea horses live on "plankton"— tiny creatures that float along with the current.

With one quick slurp,
she sucks her catch
into the end
of her snout and
swallows it whole—
sea horses don't have teeth.

To drop lower in the water, sea horses tuck in their necks and roll up their tails.

To rise higher, they uncurl themselves till they are almost as straight as pencils.

When she is big enough, Sea Horse curls up her tail and sinks to the seabed.

Sea horses cannot live where the currents are very strong. They would be swept away.

She is safer here. Her camouflage protects her,
and if a storm scoops the sea into huge waves
or passing boats send currents sweeping by,
there are plenty of things to hang on to.

Sea horses have prehensile tails, which means
they can grasp things tightly with them.

When she is even bigger, Sea Horse picks one patch of reef as her home.

She wraps her tail around a coral branch. This is her holdfast. . . . Wherever she goes, she'll keep coming back to this holdfast.

24

Male Barbour's
sea horses range over only a few
square yards. The females' range
is twice as big, or
even bigger.

In a few months,
this little sea horse
will be ready to mate.
She'll spend the rest of her
life on the reef, watching
for food, meeting
her mate, and
trying to stay
almost invisible. . . .

Barbour's sea horses can mate
by the age of six months and
are fully grown at about a year.

Who's that
peering from the coral?

Shhhh, she's a sea horse.

Index

Look up the pages to find out about all these sea horse things.
Don't forget to look at both kinds of word—**this kind** and this kind.

About the Author

Chris Butterworth loves the sea and the amazing things that live in it. "A sea horse looks as magical as a mermaid," she says, "but while mermaids are made up, sea horses really exist. We need to know as much about them as we can, so we can protect them better. Otherwise, one day sea horses might join the mermaids and exist only in stories."

About Sea Horses

The sea horses in this book are Barbour's sea horses;
you can see other kinds of sea horses on the pages
at either end of the book. Marine zoologists think there
are thirty-five sea horse species, but they may still find others.
Many kinds of sea horses need protecting—millions die
each year when they are taken from the seas
to be sold and when humans disturb
the quiet waters where they live.

About the Illustrator

John Lawrence was born by the sea and has always loved swimming and puttering
along the shore. "I had never met any sea horses," he says, "so this book has given me
the opportunity I missed. They are really exciting to draw, and I have tried to imagine
how it must be to live under the water like them."

Spotted
sea horse
(Hippocampuns kuda)

Dwarf sea horse
(Hippocampus zosterae)

Short-snouted
sea horse
*(Hippocampus
hippocampus)*

Pacific
sea horse
(Hippocampus ingens)

Thorny
sea horse
(Hippocampus histrix)

Pygmy
sea horse
(Hippocampus bargibanti)

**Lemur-tail
sea horse**
(Hippocampus mohnikei)

**Short-headed
sea horse**
(Hippocampus breviceps)

**Barbour's
sea horse**
(Hippocampus barbouri)

**Zebra
sea horse**
(Hippocampus zebra)

**Long-snouted
sea horse**
(Hippocampus guttulatus)

**Great
sea horse**
(Hippocampus kelloggi)

CHRIS BUTTERWORTH is the author of more than seventy nonfiction books for children on such diverse subjects as influenza and giant squids. She says, "I wanted to write about sea horses just because they look so strange and wonderful, but as I learned more about them, I realized what mysterious and amazing tiny creatures they are."

JOHN LAWRENCE is the author-illustrator of *This Little Chick,* named by the *New York Times Book Review* as one of the ten Best Illustrated Children's Books of the Year. He says, "I had no idea that a sea horse's life was quite so strange until I started to illustrate this book. It's been really exciting to meet *Hippocampus barbouri.*"